My first book of planet

the solar system for kids

Copyright © 2022 by M.J.Parkerson

Mercury Venus Earth Mars	Jupiter Saturn Uran Neptune
Sun Moon Stars	Pluto Ceres Haumea Makemake Eris

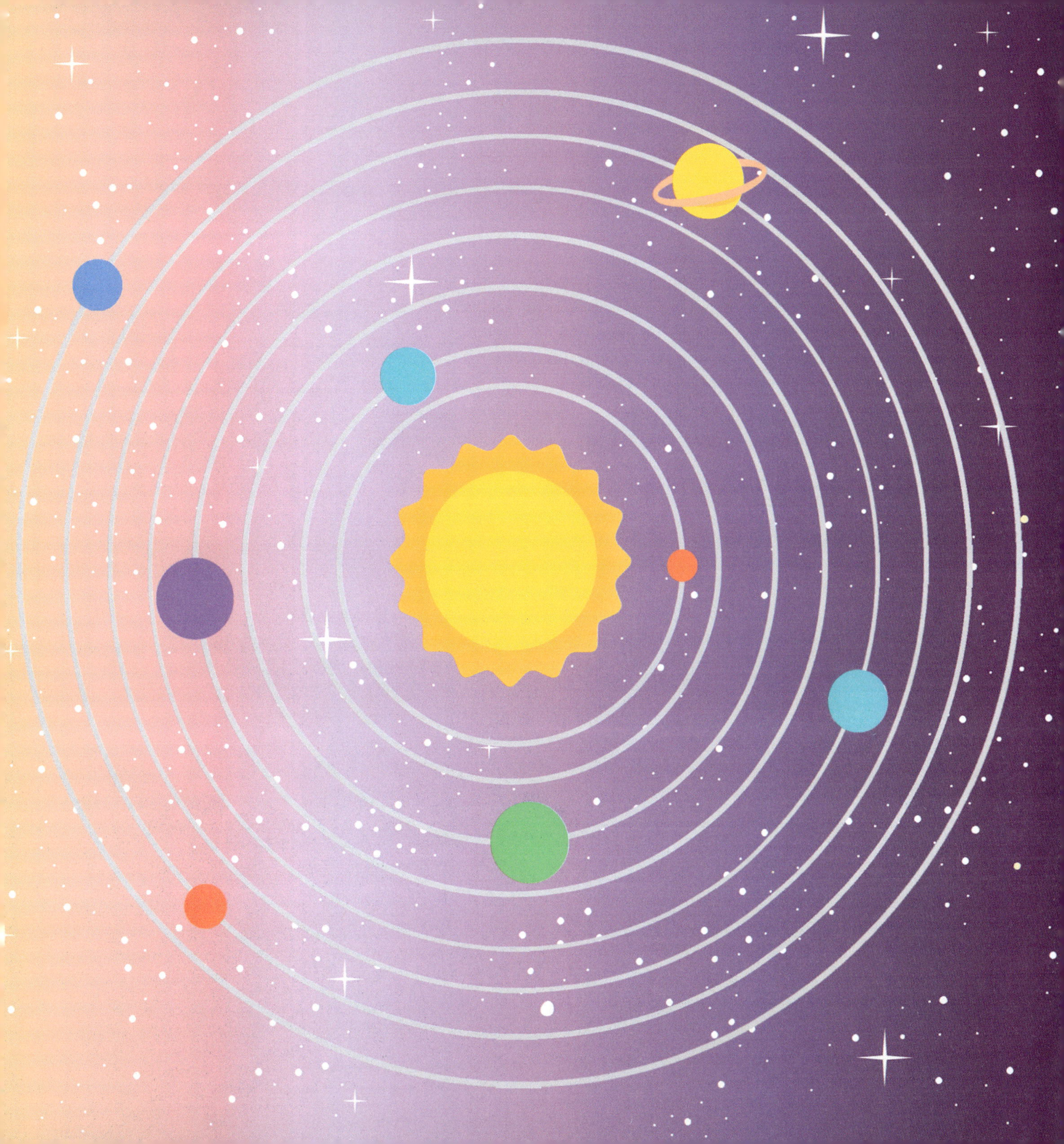

I am the first planet from the sun.

Mercury

I am the second planet from the sun.

Venus

I am the **third** planet from the sun.

Earth

I am the fourth planet from the sun.

Mars

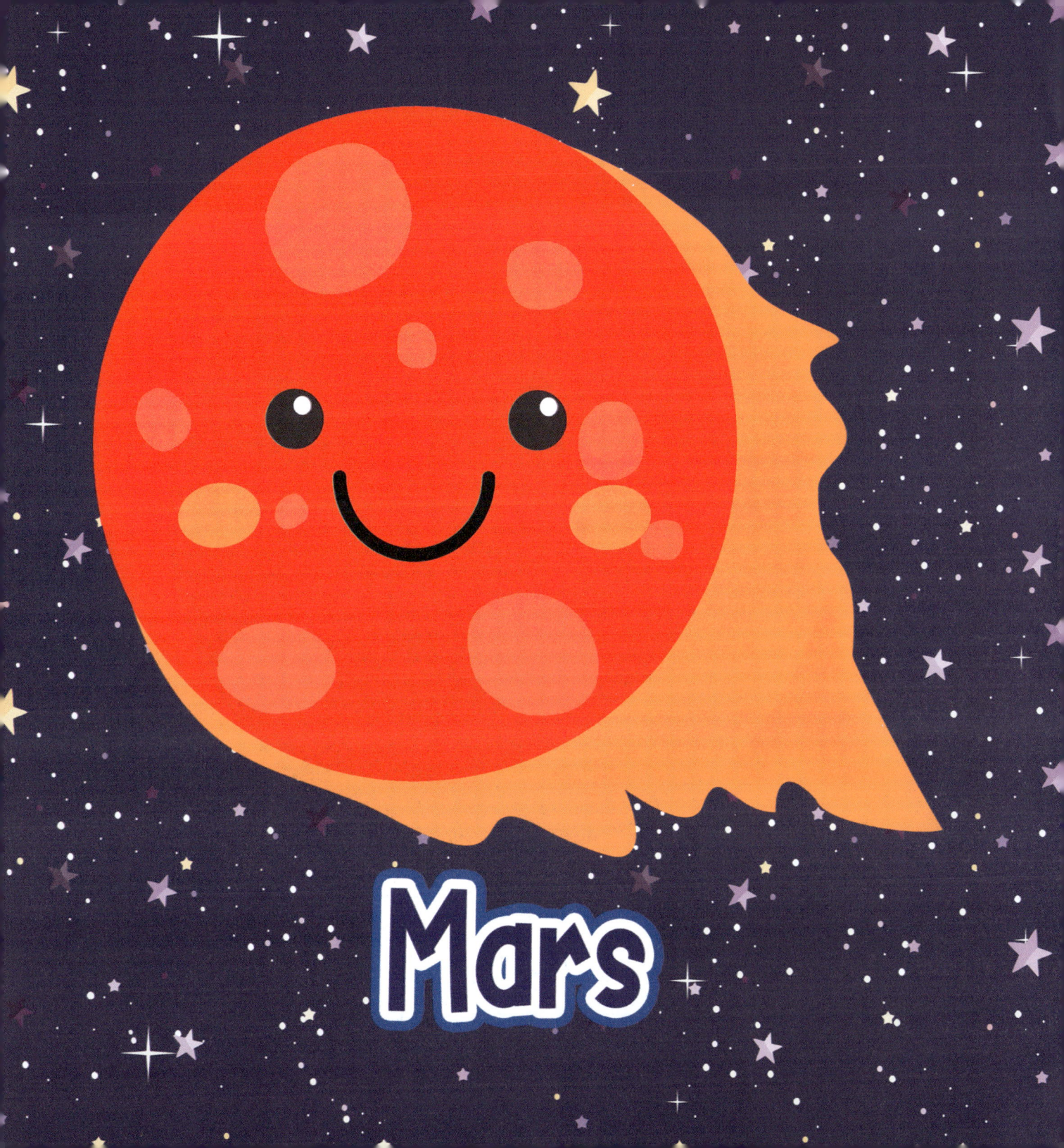

I am the fifth planet from the sun.

Jupiter

I am the sixth planet from the sun.

Saturn

I am the seventh planet from the sun.

Uranus

I am the eighth planet from the sun.

Neptune

I am the central star of the solar system.

Sun

I am the only natural satellite of the Earth.

Moon

Dwarf planets

Pluto

Ceres

Haumea

Makemake

Eris

We are giant, glowing balls of gases.

Stars

Printed in Great Britain
by Amazon